Border Terrier Dog

Your Small but Mighty Hunting Companion

Copyright © 2021

All rights reserved.

DEDICATION

The author and publisher have provided this e-book to you for your personal use only. You may not make this e-book publicly available in any way. Copyright infringement is against the law. If you believe the copy of this e-book you are reading infringes on the author's copyright, please notify the publisher at: https://us.macmillan.com/piracy

Contents

Overview 1

History 7

Appearance 10

Temperament 14

Living Needs 21

Caring for A Border Terrier 23

Health 31

Coat Color and Grooming 38

Choosing A Border Terrier Breeder 42

Average Cost to Keep for Border Terrier 47

How to Identify Border Terrier 49

Border Terrier Dog

terrier contenders for a family pet.

The Border Terrier may be small — 15 pounds or less — but he's neither tiny nor fragile. He'll happily roughhouse with kids, and he's athletic enough to keep up with anyone, which is why he's one of the few terriers well represented at such canine competitions as agility. Border owners also compete with their dogs in obedience, agility, and the show ring.

If you want a stellar companion, give him the opportunity to get out and run, smell, walk, and play a couple times a day — preferably behind a fence or on a leash, because he's definitely fast when it comes to chasing creatures like squirrels and neighborhood cats. The Border Terrier is a people dog who's prone to make a lot of noise and a big mess if left to his own devices, so he needs to live indoors as a member of the family.

Other Quick Facts

Overview

Although he's not as flashy in appearance as some of his terrier relatives, the Border Terrier is still pure terrier, living life with great gusto, whether out and about with people or digging a hole in a flowerbed. Frankly, it's a bit surprising that he isn't more popular, given that he's one of the healthier purebred dogs, is less driven to hunt than most other terriers, and is fairly flexible about exercise. He's robust, sturdy, and great with children, making him one of the top

Border Terrier Dog

The Border Terrier is characterized by his rough coat, "otter"-shaped head, and an "at the alert" attitude.

As a breed, the Border Terrier has changed little over the years, aside from becoming more consistent in appearance.

Border Terriers have thick, loose skin, which protects them from adversary bites.

Border Terrier Dog

Highlights

Border Terriers become overweight easily, so be sure to measure your Border's food and give him at least a half hour of vigorous exercise each day.

Border Terriers thrive when they're with their people and aren't meant to live outdoors with little human interaction. When left to their own devices, they can be noisy and destructive.

These escape artists will find the way out of a fenced yard if given the time and opportunity. They've been known to climb over and dig under fences, and once they get out they have little street sense to keep them from dashing out in front of cars.

Border Terriers have a high threshold for pain. If your dog's sick, the only sign may be a behavioral change, such as the dog becoming withdrawn or quiet.

Border Terriers have a natural instinct to dig. Rather than fighting it, give your Border Terrier a place of his own to dig or put his digging drive to work with fun games.

Border Terriers are active and bouncy. They love jumping up on people to greet them.

The Border Terrier's coat needs weekly brushing and periodic stripping — removing the dead hair by hand or with a stripping tool — to maintain its trademark rough texture.

Border Terriers love to chew. Some will grow out of chewing inappropriate items such as furniture and shoes, but others enjoy chewing throughout their lives. Giving them plenty of appropriate chew toys is the best way to avoid expensive replacements and unnecessary vet bills.

Border Terriers aren't yappy, but they'll bark to alert you of anything unusual, and they can become nuisance barkers if they get bored.

Border Terriers have a high prey drive and will chase, attack, and even kill neighborhood cats, squirrels or other small animals. They'll also go after small pets such as rabbits, mice, or gerbils. Because of their tendency to chase, make sure your yard is securely fenced, and don't let your Border off leash in an unfenced area.

Border Terriers do well with other dogs and with family cats if the cat is raised with the Border Terrier or lived in the home before the Border

Border Terrier Dog

Terrier.

Border Terriers can make excellent companions for kids, but they can be rambunctious, especially when young, and can unintentionally hurt small children.

To get a healthy dog, never buy a puppy from a puppy mill, a pet store, or a breeder who doesn't provide health clearances or guarantees. Look for a reputable breeder who tests her breeding dogs to make sure they're free of genetic diseases that they might pass onto the puppies and who breeds for sound temperaments.

History

The Border Terrier originated in northeast England, near the border with Scotland, during the 18th century. He's a result of the neverending battle between farmers and foxes. Borders were built to have a long, narrow, flexible body, the better to squeeze through narrow holes and flush foxes out of their hiding places, and legs long enough to follow the horses during a foxhunt.

Of course, they had stamina to spare, a weather-resistant coat, and thick, loose skin that wasn't easily pierced by the teeth of their foxy adversaries. Early evidence of the breed includes a 1754 painting by Arthur Wentworth of two Border Terriers.

While he was prized in England's border country for his fearless and implacable nature, the Border Terrier was little known elsewhere. You would certainly have seen him at agricultural shows in Northumberland in the late 19th century, but on the whole dog fanciers took little notice of him until the early 20th century. In 1920, he was recognized by England's Kennel Club, and a breed club was formed.

The first Border Terrier registered in the United States was Netherbyers Ricky, in 1930. For most of his existence, the Border Terrier has been an unknown, and his people prefer that he stay that way if it means protecting him from the ravages of popularity. Currently, he ranks 81st among the 155 breeds and varieties registered by the American Kennel Club.

Border Terrier Dog

Appearance

Height at the withers: Males 33 - 40 cm, Females 28 - 36 cm

Average Weight: Males 6.0 - 7.0 kg, Females 5.0 - 6.5 kg

The Border Terrier is perfectly built for the job they were bred to do. They are compact, sturdy and well put together terriers that boast an incredible amount of stamina. These little terriers boast very "otter-like" heads with a broadish skull and strong looking, short muzzle. Border Terriers typically have black noses although flesh or liver colours are acceptable as a breed standard too.

They have keen, alert eyes and a strong jaw line with a perfect bite. Their necks are well-proportioned in comparison to the rest of their bodies which are narrow and long with their ribcage being quite far back which are never too broad. They have rangy hindquarters and small feet with nicely formed, thick pads. Border Terriers are long in the leg as compared to other terriers which is one of their distinguishing physical traits. Their short tail is thicker at the base tapering off at the tip which these little dogs carry high.

Border Terriers have coarse, dense top coats with a close, softer undercoat and they have very thick skin. When it comes to acceptable Kennel Club breed colours, these are as follows:

Blue & Tan

Border Terrier Dog

Dark Grizzle

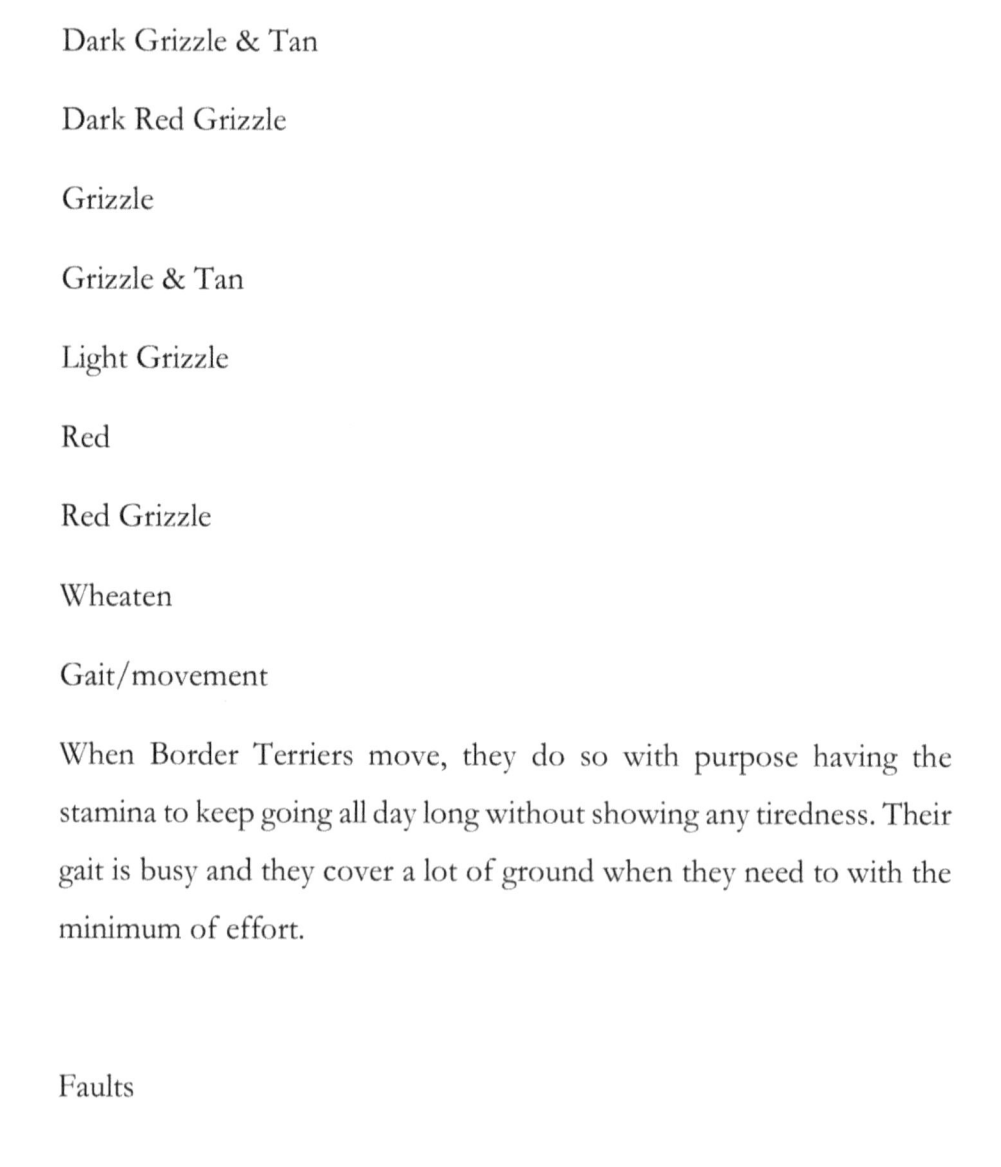

Dark Grizzle & Tan

Dark Red Grizzle

Grizzle

Grizzle & Tan

Light Grizzle

Red

Red Grizzle

Wheaten

Gait/movement

When Border Terriers move, they do so with purpose having the stamina to keep going all day long without showing any tiredness. Their gait is busy and they cover a lot of ground when they need to with the minimum of effort.

Faults

Border Terrier Dog

The Kennel Club frowns on any exaggerations or departures from the breed standard and the seriousness of the fault would be judged on how much it affects a dog's overall health and wellbeing as well as their ability to perform.

Male Border Terriers must have both testicles fully descended into their scrotums and it is worth noting that the size of a Border Terrier can be a little smaller or slight bigger as well as being a little taller or slightly shorter than stated in their Kennel Club breed standard which is to be used only as a guide for the breed.

Temperament

Border Terriers are not like other terrier-types to look at or in nature. Their raggedy appearance disguises well their affectionate, loveable albeit independent natures with their cheeky, otter-like looks. They are often described as being "energetic terriers known for their gameness"

which is a very good way of describing these little dogs because they do need to be kept busy to be truly happy and well-balanced characters. Border Terriers retain their strong instinct to chase down prey and like nothing better than to be outdoors doing what they do best which is just that. With this said, providing they are given enough to do and lots of physical exercise, they fit in well as a family pet and thrive in a home environment.

As with other terriers and dogs in general, the Border Terrier really does need to be well-socialised from a young age so they get on with other animals commonly kept as family pets and this includes cats. However, if a neighbour's cat ventures into their territory, a Border Terrier would see them as "fair game" and would not be able to resist chasing a visiting cat off the property.

Border Terriers are intelligent little dogs which means they learn things quickly both the good and the "bad". They can be a little stubborn at times and if they think there is something more interesting to do, they are more than likely to ignore a command and go off and do their own thing. On top of this, because the Border Terrier boasts a high prey drive, it's important for gardens to be made very secure because these little dogs will try to get over or under a fence when the mood takes them. They are known to be highly skilled escape artists.

Although hardy, the Border Terrier is a sensitive character and responds well to positive reinforcement training. These terriers do not respond well to any harsh handling. Their training needs to start as early as possible when puppies are at their most receptive and their education must continue throughout their lives to remind them of their place in the pack which typically needs gently doing from time to time.

Border Terriers are very good at agility all thanks to their active and lively natures. This paired to the fact they love nothing more than to be kept busy, means they excel at canine sporting activities like Flyball, loving every minute of the attention they are given when they take part in any competitions.

Border Terrier Dog

Are they a good choice for first time owners?

Border Terriers although affectionate and kind by nature are not the best choice for first time dog owners because they need to be trained and socialised by people who are familiar with their specific needs, bearing in mind that Border Terriers are truly working dogs which is a trait that is deeply embedded in their psyche.

What about prey drive?

Border Terrier Dog

Border Terriers have an extremely high prey drive and would be quick off the mark when they spot any smaller animals or pets which they would consider as fair "game". As such, care should always be taken as to where and when a Border Terrier can run free off their leads when out in a public place.

What about playfulness?

Border Terriers are known to be real comedians when the mood takes them and enjoy playing lots of interactive games. They are particularly good at sporting activities which includes agility which they thoroughly enjoy more especially as it typically involves running through tunnels.

What about adaptability?

Border Terriers are adaptable little dogs, but they do a whole lot better living in the country environment or in a house with a large back garden providing the fencing is ultra-secure which cannot be stressed strongly enough where these little terriers are concerned. Given that they need a tremendous amount of daily exercise and mental stimulation, a Border Terrier would not be as happy living in an apartment in town or being left to their own devices for any length of time.

What about separation anxiety?

Border Terriers form strong ties with their families and owners which means they hate being left on their own for any length of time which can result in a dog suffering from separation anxiety. This can lead to a dog developing unwanted and destructive behaviours around the home.

What about excessive barking?

When unhappy or left to their own devices, a Border Terrier would show their displeasure at the situation by barking incessantly which is their way of getting the attention they thrive on. With this said, they can be taught not to bark unnecessarily providing this part of their education starts early and dogs are not told off too harshly when they do bark. The reason being that Border Terriers might be robust but they are sensitive by nature and therefore do not respond well to harsh words or correction.

Do Border Terriers Like Water?

Some Border Terriers like water although they are not the best "swimmers". Other dogs hate water and it would be a mistake to force a Border Terrier to take a swim because it would end up frightening them even more.

Are Border Terriers good watchdogs?

A Border Terrier would be quick to let an owner know when there are strangers around or when they are unhappy about a situation and being so tenacious and bold, they are known to be good watchdogs protecting their families and properties without hesitation at all.

Living Needs

Border terriers don't need a lot of space and are perfectly happy living in apartments, so long as you meet their exercise requirements. A good walk for 30 minutes a day may be sufficient. But if you love long hikes or runs through the park, you can bet that your border terrier will love bounding along beside you. Their strong prey drive does mean that border terriers are not great off-leash companions. "They were originally bred to go after foxes and hunt rats, and the problem with that is they don't pay attention to anything around them when they're on the hunt," Ott says.

Despite their petite size, they can be both high jumpers and single-minded diggers, so if you plan to leave your dog in the yard unattended you'll need to account for those issues. It's best to build your fence high and have it run deep to stop them from escaping and running off after a squirrel or rabbit.

These dogs do not tend to do well left alone for long periods of time, and want to be with their owners as much as possible. As much as they love being active, they're more than happy to cuddle up on a lap and just chill too (especially as they get older and lose some of their puppy rambunctiousness).

Caring for A Border Terrier

As with any other breed, Border Terriers need to be groomed on a regular basis to make sure their coats and skin are kept in tip-top condition. They also need to be given regular daily exercise to make sure they remain fit and healthy. On top of this, these little dogs need to be fed a good quality diet and one that meets all their nutritional needs throughout their lives.

Caring for an Border Terrier puppy

Border Terrier puppies are very cute and they are also extremely smart which means it is essential for homes and gardens to be puppy-proofed to ensure they stay safe when they arrive in their new homes. Even puppies are tenacious and will find the weakness point in a fence when they want to because Border Terriers are extremely good "escape artists". It is a good idea to dig in some chicken wire around fences which is a good way of preventing a puppy from digging their way out of a garden. Fences also need to be quite high, because Border Terriers are excellent "climbers" too.

All puppies like to chew on things and this includes the Border Terrier so it's essential that all electric wires and cables are well out of a puppy's reach just in case they decide to gnaw on them. It's also important to set up a quiet area for a puppy so that when they want to take a nap, they can retreat to it bearing in mind that puppies need a lot of sleep which can be up to 21 hours a day. If there are any children in the house, they should be taught when to leave a puppy alone which is when they are eating and sleeping.

Border Terrier puppies are not difficult to house train because they are smart and quickly learn where to do their business. However, if a puppy does have an "accident" it's best not to tell them off too harshly because Border Terriers are sensitive by nature and it could end up having an adverse effect on them.

The documentation a breeder provides for a puppy must have all the details of their worming date and the product used as well as the information relating to their microchip. It is essential for puppies to be wormed again keeping to a schedule which is as follows:

Puppies should be wormed at 6 months old

They need to be wormed again when they are 8 months old

Border Terrier Dog

Puppies should be wormed when they are 10 months old

They need to be wormed when they are 12 months old

Things you'll need for your puppy

There are items needed to care for a puppy which should be purchased well in advance of their arrival. The items needed include the following:

Feed and water bowls making sure they are not too deep and ideally, they should be ceramic rather than plastic or metal

A good quality dog collar, harness and lead

A dog crate that's not too small or too big that a puppy would feel lost in it

A well-made dog bed bearing in mind that a puppy could well chew on it

Baby and/or dog blankets to use in the puppy's crate and dog bed

Dog specific toothpaste and tooth brush

Good quality toys and chews for puppies to play with and gnaw on

Shampoo and conditioner specifically formulated for use on dogs

Grooming equipment

Keeping the noise down

All puppies are very sensitive to loud noises so it is important to keep the volume of a television down and not to play music too loudly either because it could frighten a Border Terrier puppy and prevent them from napping as they should during the day.

Keeping vet appointments

Reputable breeders would always ensure their puppies vaccinated before they are sold, but as previously mentioned, it is up to their new owners to make sure they are given their follow-up shots at the right time which should be as follows:

10 -12 weeks old, bearing in mind that a puppy would not have full protection straight away, but would only be fully protected 2 weeks after they have had their second vaccination

Border Terrier Dog

When it comes to boosters, it's best to discuss these with a vet because there is a lot of debate about whether a dog really needs them after a certain time. However, if a dog ever needed to go into kennels, their vaccinations would need to be

What about Border Terriers when they reach their golden years?

When Border Terriers reach their golden years, they slow down in certain ways and might start showing their age with more grey hairs appearing on their faces and more especially around their muzzles. Apart from a change in their appearance, owners often notice a change in a dog's personality too and this includes on how quickly they respond to a command or when their names are called. The reason for this is that many older dog's hearing is not as good as it once was. Other changes to watch out for could include the following:

Their vision might be impaired and their eyes seem cloudy

Their teeth might not be as in good condition which means they may need dental work

Older dogs tend to sleep more during the day and they get up more frequently at night which is often because their cognitive function is not as sharp as it was when they were young which means older dogs are more easily confused

They tend to be less tolerant of loud noises and sounds

Dogs when they are older can be a little fussier about their food so it's important to rethink their diet and to make sure they are getting all the nutrients they need to stay healthy

An older dog's immune system often does not offer them the same protection against illness and infection which puts them more at risk of catching something and why they should see the vet more routinely

An older dog might not be so keen to go out for a walk and more especially longer ones

They muscle tone and body condition is not as good as when they were young

Older dogs often suffer from joint problems which can then lead to arthritis so it's well worth investing in a comfy dog bed and ideally one that a dog finds easier to get out of

Health

Border Terriers are generally healthy, but like all breeds, they can get certain health conditions. Not all Border Terriers will get any or all of these diseases, but it's important to be aware of them if you're considering this breed.

If you're buying a puppy, find a good breeder who will show you health clearances for both your puppy's parents. Health clearances prove that a dog's been tested for and cleared of a particular condition.

In Border Terriers, you should expect to see health clearances from the Orthopedic Foundation for Animals for hips and from the Canine Eye Registry Foundation (CERF) certifying that the eyes are normal.

Because some health problems don't appear until a dog reaches full maturity, health clearances aren't issued to dogs younger than 2 years old. Look for a breeder who doesn't breed her dogs until they're two or three years old.

The following problems are not common in the breed, but they may occur:

Hip Dysplasia is a condition in which the femur doesn't fit snugly into the pelvic socket of the hip joint. Hip dysplasia can exist with or without clinical signs. Some dogs exhibit pain and lameness on one or both rear legs. As the dog ages, arthritis can develop. Screening for hip dysplasia can be done by the Orthopedic Foundation for Animals (OFA) or the University of Pennsylvania Hip Improvement Program (PennHIP). Dogs who have hip dysplasia shouldn't be bred. If your dog displays signs of hip dysplasia, talk to your vet. Medication or surgery can help.

Heart defects of various kinds can affect Border Terriers, the most common of which is pulmonic stenosis, a narrowing of the valve that separates the right chamber of the heart from the lungs. If your Border Terrier has a heart murmur, it may indicate that he has a heart condition that will need to be monitored and treated. Heart murmurs are caused by a disturbance in the blood flow through the chambers of the heart. They're graded on their loudness, with one being very soft and six being very loud. If disease is evident, as diagnosed through xrays and an echocardiogram, the dog may require medication, a special diet, and a reduction in the amount of exercise he gets. The best way to avoid heart defects is to check that the breeder has not used dogs with heart defects in her breeding program.

Malocclusions, meaning the dog's jaws don't fit together correctly, are sometimes found in Border Terriers. There are three different types of incorrect bites. An overshot bite is when the upper jaw extends past the lower jaw. This causes difficulties in grasping; in more severe cases, the lower teeth can bite into the roof of the mouth, causing serious injuries. An undershot bite is when the lower jaw extends out past the upper jaw. Although it is standard in some breeds, it can cause difficulties in Border Terriers and may need to be corrected with surgery. The last type of incorrect bite is wry mouth, a twisting of the mouth caused when one side grows more quickly than the other. It causes difficulties with eating and grasping. In some cases, puppies grow out of these incorrect bites, but if the bite hasn't become normal by the time the puppy is 10 months old, it may need to be corrected surgically. If this is the case, wait until the puppy has finished growing.

Corrective surgeries can include tooth extraction, crown height reductions, or the use of spacers. Dogs with incorrect bites, even if the bite is corrected surgically, should not be used for breeding.

Seizures can be caused by a number of factors and can occur at any time. Signs of a seizure include sudden trembling or shaking, sudden urination, stiffness, staring, slight muscle spasms, or a loss of consciousness. Seizures aren't curable, but they can be successfully managed with medication.

Patellar Luxation, also known as "slipped stifles," is a common problem in small dogs. It is caused when the patella, which has three parts-the femur (thigh bone), patella (knee cap), and tibia (calf)-is not properly lined up. This causes lameness in the leg or an abnormal gait, sort of like a skip or a hop. It is a condition that is present at birth although the actual misalignment or luxation does not always occur until much later. The rubbing caused by patellar luxation can lead to arthritis, a degenerative joint disease. There are four grades of patellar luxation, ranging from grade I, an occasional luxation causing temporary lameness in the joint, to grade IV, in which the turning of the tibia is severe and the patella cannot be realigned manually. This gives the dog a bowlegged appearance. Severe grades of patellar luxation may require surgical repair.

Hypothyroidism occurs when the body can't maintain sufficient levels of thyroid hormones. Signs include weight gain, thinning coat, dry skin, slow heart rate, and sensitivity to cold. As hypothyroidism is a progressive condition, if you notice any of these signs, have your dog checked by your vet. Hypothyroidism is easily managed with daily medication, which must continue throughout the dog's life. Because this is a disease of middle age, asking the breeder about the thyroid status of your puppy's grandparents may give you a better idea of whether the problem occurs in the breeder's lines.

Cryptorchidism is a condition in which one or both testicles on the dog fail to descend and is common in small dogs. Testicles should descend fully by the time the puppy is 2 months old. If a testicle is retained, it is usually nonfunctional and can become cancerous if it is not removed. When the neutering takes place, a small incision is made to remove the undescended testicle(s); the normal testicle, if any, is removed in the regular manner.

Coat Color and Grooming

The Border Terrier has a short, dense undercoat covered with a wiry topcoat. His skin is thick and loose — something that came in handy during his fox-hunting days, as it protects him from bites.

The Border Terrier coat can be red, blue and tan, grizzle and tan, or wheaten (pale yellow or fawn). Some have a small patch of white on the chest.

Weekly brushing and periodic stripping (every five to six months) of the rough terrier coat will keep your Border looking neat and tidy. Your grooming kit should include a fine comb, a natural bristle brush, and a stripping knife (unless you opt for having a professional groomer take care of stripping the coat).

Stripping involves plucking the dead hair by hand or removing it with a stripping knife or other stripping tool. It's the kind of thing you can do while you and your Border are watching a 30-minute television show. Your Border's breeder can show you how to strip the coat, or you can find a professional groomer who knows how to do it — not all do. You'll find that by stripping the coat, you'll have less Border hair decorating your clothing, furniture, and flooring.

For easier care, you can clipper the coat, but the texture and color will become softer and lighter and the coat won't be weather resistant.

If you don't mind the scruffy look, you can just leave the coat as is, with no stripping or clipping, but the coat may shed more.

Border Terriers do not need to be bathed often — only when they've gotten into something gross and it's really necessary. Their coat naturally repels dirt and, with weekly brushing and a wipe-down with a damp cloth when needed, it should stay fairly clean. When you do bathe him, use a shampoo made for the rough terrier coat to help maintain its texture.

Brush your Border Terrier's teeth at least two or three times a week to remove tartar buildup and the accompanying bacteria. Daily is better. Trim his nails once or twice a month, as needed. If you can hear the nail clicking on the floor, they're too long. Short nails keep the feet in good condition, don't get caught in the carpet and tear, and don't scratch your legs when your Border Terrier enthusiastically jumps up to greet you.

Start grooming your Border when he's a puppy to get him used to it. Handle his paws frequently — dogs are touchy about their feet — and look inside his mouth and ears. Make grooming a positive experience filled with praise and rewards, and you'll lay the groundwork for easy veterinary exams and other handling when he's an adult.

Choosing A Border Terrier Breeder

Selecting a respected breeder is the key to finding the right puppy. Reputable breeders will welcome questions about temperament and health clearances, as well as explain the history of the breed and what kind of puppy makes for a good pet. Don't be shy about describing exactly what you're looking for in a dog — breeders interact with their puppies daily and can make accurate recommendations once they know something about your lifestyle and personality.

Lots of breeders have websites, so how can you tell who's good and who's not? Red flags to look out for: multiple litters on the premises, puppies always being available, having your choice of any puppy, and being offered the option to pay online with a credit card. Breeders who sell puppies at a lower price "without papers" are unethical and should be reported to the American Kennel Club. You should also bear in mind that buying a puppy from websites that offer to ship your dog to you immediately can be a risky venture, as it leaves you no recourse if what you get isn't exactly what you expected. Put at least as much effort into researching your puppy as you would into choosing a new car or expensive appliance. It will save you money in the long run.

To start your search, check out the website of the Border Terrier Club of America and select a breeder who has agreed to abide by the

BTCA's ethical standard, which specifies that members not place puppies prior to 12 weeks of age, prohibits the sale of puppies through pet stores, and calls for the breeder to obtain recommended health clearances before breeding.

Whether you're planning to get your new best friend from a breeder, a pet store, or another source, don't forget that old adage "let the buyer beware". Disreputable breeders and facilities that deal with puppy mills can be hard to distinguish from reliable operations. There's no 100%

guaranteed way to make sure you'll never purchase a sick puppy, but researching the breed (so you know what to expect), checking out the facility (to identify unhealthy conditions or sick animals), and asking the right questions can reduce the chances of heading into a disastrous situation. And don't forget to ask your veterinarian, who can often refer you to a reputable breeder, breed rescue organization, or other reliable source for healthy puppies.

The cost of a Border Terrier puppy varies depending on the breeder's locale, the sex of the puppy, the titles (ideally working or hunting) that the puppy's parents have, and whether the puppy is best suited for the show ring or a pet home. Puppies should be temperament tested, vetted, dewormed, and socialized to give them a healthy, confident start in life. If you put as much effort into researching your puppy as you would when buying a new car, it will save you money in the long run.

Before you decide to buy a puppy, consider whether an adult Border Terrier may better suit your lifestyle. Puppies are loads of fun, but they require a good deal of time and effort before they grow up to be the dog of your dreams. An adult may already have some training, and he'll probably be less active, destructive, and demanding than a puppy. With an adult, you know more about what you're getting in terms of personality and health and you can find adults through breeders or shelters. If you are interested in acquiring an older dog through breeders, ask them about purchasing a retired show dog or if they know of an adult dog who needs a new home. If you want to adopt a dog, read the advice below on how to do that.

Average Cost to Keep for Border Terrier

If you are looking to buy a Border Terrier, you would need to pay anything from £450 to well over £800 for a well-bred pedigree puppy. The cost of insuring a male 3-year old Border Terrier in the north of England would be £16.77 a month for basic cover, but this rises to £38.15 a month for a lifetime policy (quote as of August 2017). It's worth bearing in mind that lots of things are factored into a dog's insurance premium and this includes where you live in the UK and their age and breed.

When it comes to food costs, you would need to buy the best quality food, whether wet or dry, for your dog throughout their lives and it must suit the different stages of their lives too. This could set you back between £25 - £35 a month. On top of this, you would need to factor in veterinary costs if you want to share your home with a Border Terrier which includes their initial vaccinations, neutering or spaying them when the time is right and then their annual health check visits, all of which can quickly add up to over a £800 a year.

As a rough guide, the total average cost to keep and care for a Border Terrier would be between £50 - £85 a month depending on the level of pet insurance you opt to buy for your dog, but this does not include the initial cost of buying a well-bred pedigree Border Terrier puppy.

How to Identify Border Terrier

Method 1: Taking Notice of Body Structure

1, Check the dog's size. Border Terriers are fairly small dogs. They are only 12–15 inches (30.5–38.1 cm) tall and males weigh 13–15 pounds (5.9–6.8 kg) whilst females weigh 11.5–14 pounds (5.2–6.4 kg).

Border Terrier Dog

2, Look at the eyes. Borders have dark hazel coloured eyes which are full of fire and intelligence. The eyes are medium sized and not too prominent or beady.

3, Notice the ears. A Border Terrier has small V-shaped ears which are medium in size and generally darker coloured. The ears aren't set high on the head, but more to the sides of the head.

4, Inspect the muzzle. Borders usually have rather short muzzles that are darker coloured. A few short whiskers are natural. They have a good-sized, black nose, and a bite which is large in proportion to the dog.

5, View the tail. Border Terriers have moderately short tails which are thick at the base. The tail isn't set too high, but it is carried brightly when the dog is alert.

6, Examine the overall structure. Border Terriers have a deep, fairly narrow body which has enough length to be agile. The shoulder blades are well laid back, meeting the withers gradually. The dog has muscular and racy hind legs with long thighs, and the feet in front.

Method 2:Recognising the Coat

1, Check the coat's texture and appearance. Border Terriers have a short dense undercoat which is covered by a wiry, somewhat broken topcoat. The wiry coat is weatherproof, and tough which protects the dog from rain, mist and rough terrain.

2, Notice the colour of the coat. Borders have a range of colours that they can be, however there are 4 different colors that are standard and approved as purebred. Any of these colours that the dog can be may have a small amount of white markings on the chest.

- The acceptable purebred coat colours for Border Terriers are red, grizzle and tan, blue and tan and wheaten.
- Other more unusual (and not recognized as purebred) coat

colours include black and red, black and tan, black grizzle, blue grizzle, grizzle, red grizzle, red grizzle and tan, and red wheaten.

Method 3: Identifying Temperament

1, Notice how playful the dog is. Border Terriers are very playful dogs, and are energetic and athletic. They tend to play rough and prefer vigorous exercise and interactive games.

2, Look for independence. Borders are independent in many ways, and may also be stubborn. The dog will want to escape any back yards or places they're in, to explore the outside world. This curiosity is something that helps them learn new tricks.

3, Watch for how social the dog is. Most Border Terriers are social dogs with both humans and other dogs. They'll usually want to greet strangers with bounciness, and will get along alright with other dogs.

4, Check the dog's reaction to other animals. Borders get along with animals they've been raised with, but any animals they might consider prey (including smaller dog breeds, like those in the toy group) are out of the question. They'll feel compelled to run and harass anything that moves quickly. Border Terriers also have a hunting background, and this will often come into play if a cat crosses their path.